# RESCUE 911™

## KID HEROES

★ ★ ★

# RESCUE 911™

## KID HEROES
☆ ☆ ☆

## Alison Hendrie

*The stories in this book are based on actual events as depicted on RESCUE 911. The names have been changed. Any similarity with real names is coincidental.*

Published by The Trumpet Club
1540 Broadway, New York, New York 10036
Text Copyright © 1992 by The Trumpet Club, Inc.

ISBN 0-440-84816-4

Produced by Neuwirth & Associates

Printed in the United States of America
November 1992

5 7 9 10 8 6 4
CWO

*Special Thanks to*
*Arnold Shapiro Productions*

# Table of Contents

✩ ✩ ✩

# Introduction

It's an average, everyday sort of day. You're walking down the street and you hear sirens wailing in the distance. You say, "Must be a fire somewhere. . . . Must be the cops chasing a burglar. . . . Sure glad it's not me. Must be another town, another family."

But emergencies sometimes do happen to kids like you and to families like yours.

Once a week on national television you can relive the terrifying and very real stories of kids just like you. Kids who have saved lives—sometimes even their own.

*Rescue 911* is that show. Like other TV shows, it's filled with action, adventure, and drama. But there's one big difference: These adventures are the real thing, and they happen to real people.

As you read these stories, you will see the bravery

of everyday people. You will experience their fear, confusion, courage, and hope. You will learn that you too, if faced with sudden disaster, *can* make a difference—alone, and with the help of professional rescue and emergency workers.

As you read, remember ... it takes three simple numbers to save lives: **Dial 9-1-1**.

*If your community does not have 911, learn the emergency numbers in your area, and post them by each phone.*

# Best Buddies

**A** friend is one of the most important people you will have in your life. It is a very special feeling to have a friend you can feel close to and share things with. It is also a special feeling to be a friend—to be able to help someone you like, and to just be there if he or she needs you.

And then of course, there's your *best* friend: the one you tell all your secrets to; the one you hang out with every day and call every night; the one with whom you laugh and giggle and fight; the one who is the most fun.

Do you have a best friend? If you do, then you know how much you trust and care for him or her. Do you feel you would do anything for your best friend? Would he or she do anything for you? Of

course. You wouldn't even need to ask. That is what
friendship is all about.

You are going to meet two friends who never
questioned their close friendship—even when it
meant doing *anything!*

Greg Crawford, eleven years old, and Ricky Larkin, also eleven, are the very best of buddies. They
live in Louisiana, and do just about everything together. It is a good thing they are such good friends,
because one bright winter afternoon last year, their
friendship was tested—and the final grade was life
or death.

On Sunday, February 24, 1991, best buddies Greg
and Ricky were playing at Greg's house when they
decided to build a fort out in the woods. Greg asked
his parents if he could borrow the hatchet (a sharp
axe-like tool that adults use to chop wood) to help
make their fort. Greg's mom, Pat, didn't like the
idea of the boys playing with a sharp hatchet. But
Wesley Crawford, Greg's dad, knew the boys were
responsible and would only use it with great care,
not play with it. He gave them permission to use
the tool.

By three-thirty that afternoon, the buddies were
off to the pine thicket. They were excited to be build-
ing their own fort and felt very grown-up doing it
all by themselves. For almost an hour and a half,
the boys were busy noisily cutting down small trees
and constructing their project, happy to be out in

the fresh air among the sweet-smelling pine needles that covered the ground around them.

At about twenty minutes to five, they decided to finish up and return home so that Ricky could get to church on time. The woods in which the half-built fort stood had a steep hill off to one side, dropping down to the street below. It had been raining for a few days, so the ground was damp and muddy. The pine needles on top of the mud were very slippery and made walking difficult, but the boys laughed and sang as they slipped and slid along the hill heading home.

Just ahead, the two friends spotted a rope hanging from a big tree at the edge of the steepest part of the hill. The boys knew the rope was used as a swing by the neighborhood kids. They would put their foot through the loop at the bottom of the rope and swing high out over the hill, as if they were flying.

Ricky was always the class clown, always making jokes and pulling funny stunts just to make people laugh. Usually he was very funny. On this day, he raced ahead of Greg and grabbed the rope, making all kinds of silly faces. Greg laughed and calmly walked after him. Ricky thought it would be funny to put the rope around his neck and pretend he was choking.

"Hey," he yelled to Greg, "I'm gonna hang myself!" Greg, who was always a little more quiet and serious than his clowning buddy, didn't think that would be funny and told Ricky to stop fooling around.

At that very moment, Greg heard some voices below him and turned to see if he knew any of the kids walking along near the football field. While Greg's back was turned, Ricky placed the rope around his neck and then slipped on the pine needles. He lost his balance and suddenly became very still.

Greg looked back to see what his friend was doing and noticed Ricky wasn't moving. His knees were bent and his back was to Greg so his face couldn't be seen. At first Greg thought his friend was fooling around again. He ran over and shook Ricky and told him to cut it out. But Ricky didn't answer. He didn't move. A blue ring was beginning to form around his mouth. At that moment Greg knew Ricky was in real trouble and that this was no joke. He was afraid Ricky would die. Greg had to get Ricky down from the tree and he had to work fast.

Remembering the hatchet, Greg grabbed it and began hacking away at the rope above Ricky's head. It felt like the chopping took forever, but finally Greg broke through the thick rope and Ricky lay on the ground. He was still unconscious and his pale face and blue mouth made Greg feel he had to do something. He realized his best friend in the world might die and the thought made him jump into action.

Greg breathlessly raced back to his house, stum-

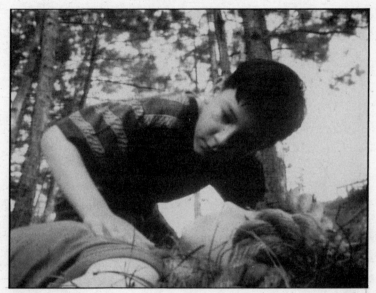

"Ricky didn't answer. He didn't move...Greg knew that
Ricky was in trouble..."

bling along the path and screaming at the top of
his lungs. His parents assumed Ricky had cut himself with the hatchet. They grabbed the car keys
and quickly drove over to the site of the accident to
see what they could do. On the drive over, Greg told
Wesley and Pat what Ricky had done. But they did
not believe it was so bad until they saw the young
boy lying motionless on the dirt. By that time, he
was having trouble breathing and his body suddenly began to convulse, to shake violently with

jerky motions. The Crawfords knew they needed emergency help—right away.

While Wesley stayed with the boys, Pat ran to the neighbors' house and dialed 911. Officer Scott Adler was patrolling nearby and picked up the call. He was on the scene in minutes, struggling up the steep, slippery hill to reach Ricky and help him.

In the meantime, the neighbors had called Ricky's mother. She too could not believe what had happened to her son. She cried and screamed so much that Officer Adler, knowing how hard it must be for a mother to see her son so badly hurt, asked Pat to take her away and calm her down. The two mothers went down to the street and cried, hugging each other for comfort.

At the top of the hill, Officer Adler checked Ricky's pulse and cleared out the boy's throat to help him breathe easier. He questioned Greg about how all this had happened. As Greg explained how Ricky had accidentally slipped with the rope around his neck, choking himself, the ambulance arrived at the scene. Paramedic Amblin, part of the emergency medical team (EMT) from the ambulance, got to work immediately. Ricky's neck was swollen and they were not sure if it was broken but they had to get him into the ambulance and to a hospital right away.

Because the hill was so slippery, the emergency team decided to carry Ricky down in their arms instead of putting him on the board they would normally use. After making sure his head wouldn't move and his neck would stay still, the emergency team began a slow, scary trip down the slope with the injured boy. Police officers surrounded the team to help in their descent and after a few tense minutes Ricky was safely placed in the ambulance.

But this was only the beginning. Ricky was seriously injured and needed to see a doctor immediately. His body continued to convulse and he was still having trouble breathing, even with the help of the air tube the medical team placed in his throat.

The ambulance raced through the streets and got Ricky to Lincoln Hospital Emergency Room at 5:00 P.M.—at just the time the boy was supposed to have been at church. The emergency-room doctors quickly got his breathing back to normal and checked his heart and other vital organs. They thought his brain might swell up like his throat had, so they gave him medicine to stabilize it (keep it normal) and to stop his convulsions.

Now that the emergency was over, the doctors had found that he had no broken bones and would not be paralyzed. But they were concerned that his brain might have gone without oxygen, which we all need in order to function, for a long time. This could be very dangerous because the brain controls everything we do and if it does not get enough oxygen, it can become damaged and will not work properly. The doctors decided Ricky should be taken by helicopter to a hospital seventy miles away, which had a special unit for children.

Ricky was taken to Schumpert Medical Center,

which has all the modern equipment and the best doctors to care for children with brain problems. But they could do nothing except wait until Ricky woke up to see if he was really okay. The first twelve hours after an injury like Ricky's are the most important, and Ricky's mother stayed by his side the entire time, watching and waiting.

Finally, after sixteen hours, Ricky opened his eyes and saw his mother. She gently asked him if he knew who she was and he brightly called her by name, wondering why she would question him and wondering what all the fuss was about. Ricky's mom was overjoyed and she knew her son was going to be just fine. After two days, Ricky was well enough to go back home and see his best buddy Greg.

Ricky had gone three or four minutes without oxygen—a long time but not enough to cause any lasting damage. The doctors agreed that if Greg had run for help before cutting the rope around Ricky's neck, Ricky would have gone much longer without air and would surely have died. Greg had saved his best friend's life.

Today the boys are never apart. They continue to play together, go to school together, and they just have fun as kids should. Ricky is lucky to have a friend like Greg and he's lucky to be playing in the sunshine with his best buddy. As Ricky says, "He saved my life and I'll always be there for him."

Ricky's mother knows that the boys have learned the true meaning of friendship from this experience as well as how to think on their feet. She is relieved to know that they are both familiar with those three important numbers: **911**.

The danger that Ricky stepped into when he was fooling around with the rope is very serious. He hanged himself with a rope that was meant to be used for a swing. Although it is fun to play outdoors, it is important to remember to be responsible and to play with things the right way:

**SWINGS**—Whether they are old-fashioned rope swings or part of a big playset, don't stand up or horse around with the ropes or chains.

**SLIDES**—Everyone loves to use the slide, so wait your turn and climb up the ladder, and don't try to walk up the front of the slide.

**MONKEY BARS**—Great fun for "swingers," but remember: do not stand on top of the bars; you might fall off or fall through the bars.

**MERRY-GO-ROUND**—Wait until it comes to a *complete* stop before trying to get on or off and be careful after a fun ride: you might be dizzy!

**PLAYGROUND EMERGENCY**—If you or one of your friends becomes seriously hurt, look for the closest adult, call a parent, and remember to **dial 9-1-1**: it could save a life!

☆ ☆ ☆

# Diabetic Dad

**W**e've all been afraid at one time or another, for all kinds of reasons: you're in an unfamiliar place; you've had a close call on your bike with an oncoming car; you're watching a scary movie; a big, angry-looking dog runs up to you.... Being afraid is an unpleasant feeling, but we can usually explain why we are frightened.

But sometimes there's another kind of fear, a tingling feeling that creeps up on you and grabs you by the roots of your hair or lies cold in the pit of your stomach. It's a quiet kind of fear, a feeling that can arise when you're in the most familiar places— your own home, for example—and with the most familiar people, like your own father.

☆ ☆ ☆

Just as the sun came up one morning last year, six-year-old Maureen Huggins awoke to a kind of quiet in her house in California. She felt that something was wrong. She could hear the faint sound of stumbling and muttering from the other room—a creepy and unfamiliar sound. Only she and her father were home at that early hour. But why was her father banging into the walls? Why was he mumbling strange things? Why was he acting so weird?

Wiping the sleep from her eyes and brushing back her long blonde hair, Maureen slid out of bed. Ever-so-cautiously she made her way to the living room, timidly peeked around the doorway and saw her father, who looked as if he didn't know where he was. He could hardly stand up and was talking as if Maureen weren't there at all. Suddenly, she didn't want to be there; she didn't want to see her own father acting so strangely. She didn't know what to expect and it scared her.

On the other side of town, 911-dispatcher Diane Booth arrived at the emergency center where she starts work every day at 6:30 A.M. It was a beautiful summer morning and Diane was feeling good. At that early hour, the emergency calls Diane usually received were just neighbors complaining about a loud party, a dog barking, or local kids making prank calls.

But on that bright July day, Diane received a call

that was none of the above: It was a true emergency.

A very young, very frightened voice on the other
end of the line begged Diane to send help to her
house right away. Little Maureen Huggins, sniffling
and shaky, cried as she told Diane that her daddy
was acting "weird" and that she was afraid of him.
Maureen knew there must be something wrong
with her father, but she had no idea what it could
be and she needed help fast. Diane could hear the
fear in her voice and could sense there was something very wrong at Maureen's house.

Diane had had a lot of experience with emergency
calls and was always quick to determine the prob-
lem and send help. But on that day, the story told
by the frightened young caller was hard to figure
out—it was a puzzle for the dispatcher. Diane's job
on that morning—possibly the most important job
she had ever had—was to unravel this mystery, and
try to save this child, and from the sound of it, to
save her father too.

As in any mystery, Diane first had to get all the
details. Keeping Maureen calm, Diane began to
question her about what was happening at home:
Was her father drunk? Had he hit her or hurt her
in any way? Was he acting violent or mean? Were
there any weapons around the house? With each
question, Diane began to dig deeper into the situation at Maureen's house. Diane was not just a dispatcher anymore; now she was also a detective.

Even though the telephone connected the two,

there was still some confusion. Diane had a hard time understanding just what Maureen was saying and she had to ask the girl to repeat herself several times before she could learn any more. In her fear and concern, Maureen was not able to communicate the important details Diane needed to know in order to send the right kind of help. The dispatcher had to proceed slowly. The call began this way:

"My dad's talking weird. He's scaring me," said Maureen.

"What's your dad's name?" Diane asked.

"Phil."

"Phil what?"

"Phil Huggins . . . Phillip Huggins."

"What's your name?"

"Maureen."

"Maureen Huggins?"

"Maureen Ann Huggins."

Those were easy questions, but Diane still could not explain the fear she heard in Maureen's voice. She was becoming increasingly concerned for Maureen's safety, and could only imagine what terrible things were happening across town to the frightened child, since she wasn't able to get the information she needed.

Like putting pieces of a puzzle together, Diane began to form a picture from Maureen's all-too-few clues. Phil Huggins had not been mean or abusive to his daughter. It sounded to Diane like he was very sick. Getting these tiny bits of information was

slow and agonizing. Diane was very patient with
Maureen but there were still some misunder-
standings:

"What is he doing now, Maureen?"

"He's drooling."

"He's drilling? What does that mean, drilling?"

"I don't know."

"You don't know what that means but you know
he's drilling?"

"Saliva is coming out of his mouth."

"Oh, he's *drooling*!"

Recognizing the urgent need for an ambulance,
Diane dispatched one right away. But she kept
Maureen on the phone. The mystery was not yet
solved.

Maureen's dad was barely conscious and lay still
on the couch, sweating and pale. Though she was
only six years old, Maureen could tell that her father was very sick and she clung to the telephone
as if it were her lifeline. She wanted to run from
her house and drag someone back to help her father.
But she knew the ambulance would be there soon.

Three minutes later, which seemed like forever
to little Maureen, she heard the wailing sirens
outside the house. Help had come at last! Maureen
dropped the phone, sprinted to the door, and ex-
citedly let Officer Garner into the now-quiet house.
On his first look, Officer Garner was almost certain
the girl's father was dead—the man's eyes were
closed, he was lying very still, and he didn't seem
to be breathing. The police officer shook Maureen's

dad. There was no response. Whatever was wrong with Maureen's dad was still a mystery. Solving it would take more time and some real detective work.

The emergency medical team arrived on the scene soon after Officer Garner and together they searched for clues to Phil Huggins' illness. It was clear the man was very ill indeed, and one look at poor frightened Maureen convinced the team that they had to hurry. Maureen was a little confused with all the people running around, but she knew they were going to help her father so she tried to be brave.

With five or six bustling emergency workers hot on the trail, it was only a few seconds before the mystery was solved: A paramedic discovered a tag hanging from Phil's neck—an identification tag that said he was a diabetic.

Diabetes is a disease people have when there is too much or too little sugar in their blood and the body doesn't know what to do with it. In Phil's case, the amount of sugar in his blood was much too low, causing him to faint—to go into diabetic shock.

After a quick test, paramedics saw that he had almost no blood sugar. His body had just "shut down"—stopped working. When this happened, first he had begun to act "weird"—stumbling around and talking funny, as Maureen had noticed earlier—until finally he became unconscious. If the emergency team hadn't arrived as soon as it did, his body would have shut off completely—and he might have died. Luckily for her father, Maureen had thought quickly and dialed 911 when she realized he was acting strange.

The paramedics pulled out a large needle and with quick, sure hands gave Phil a big shot of dextrose—a substance just like sugar—to wake him up and make sure he would be okay. Dextrose goes right to the brain and allows it to begin working normally again, which it did.

Slowly and groggily, Phil's eyes fluttered open. He blankly looked around the room at first, not sure of where he was. Then, seeing all the strange faces looking at him with concern, he shook his head and asked what had happened. His mouth was dry and sticky and he looked very tired, but other than that, he seemed to bounce right back. The worst was over. Phil was going to be okay.

Maureen, seeing her daddy awake and all right, broke into a huge smile and ran into his arms, planting a big kiss on his cheek. Phil had never been so happy to see his daughter. To Phil Huggins, his little girl was truly a hero.

Maureen's mom was also very proud of her daughter and was glad to have taught Maureen those important numbers—911. According to Mrs. Huggins and Maureen, "All parents should teach their children to call 911."

Mrs. Huggins had done the right thing in telling her daughter how to dial 911. She had communicated the importance of an emergency to Maureen and made sure the girl knew what to do. Communication is our only way of understanding each other and without it, we can be left confused and scared.

Maureen's dad should have told his daughter that he had a disease like diabetes. Not everyone looks and acts sick when they have an illness. Some illnesses are hard to spot, or they don't show any signs until it is too late. Maureen learned a hard lesson when she found her father unconscious and near death.

Diabetes is one of those hidden diseases that you may be unaware of until an emergency occurs. Phil always wears a special tag so that in case of an emergency, paramedics know what to do. If Maureen had known about his diabetes, she could have alerted the dispatcher and removed some of the confusion. But thank goodness Phil had his tag; the paramedics saw it and were able to treat him immediately.

During Maureen's telephone call with the dispatcher, it was also important to communicate to Diane exactly what was happening so the dispatcher could send the proper help. Maureen, being so young and afraid, had difficulty with many of the important details and turned the emergency into a mystery. Fortunately for everybody, the emergency team solved it and got Phil back on his feet.

If you ever think you are in an emergency situation, remember to do the following:

**LOOK FOR WARNING SIGNS**—Not all illnesses are easy to spot, but there are some signs to look for that might mean a person needs help:

- You can't wake someone up at all.
- The person is sweating and is very pale.
- The person can't speak properly or at all.
- The person acts "strange," not like himself or doesn't know where he is.
- There is serious vomiting or bleeding.

**COMMUNICATE WITH YOUR FAMILY OR AN ADULT**—The moment you think someone is hurt or sick, tell the nearest adult.

**CALL 911**—The quickest way of getting help is through 911, and be sure to tell the dispatcher everything that is happening and give as many details as you can.

☆ ☆ ☆

# Sinking Sisters Saved

**W**ould you believe that water makes up almost three-quarters of the earth's surface? Or that ninety percent of our very own bodies is actually made up of water? As strange as that might sound, it's true. Water is a very important part of our world and our lives.

It also plays an important part in having fun. A cool, clear lake; a salty, foaming ocean; a warm, bubbling bath—water gives us hours of splashing, swimming, and good clean fun.

But water can also bring danger, especially to young children and to *anyone* who doesn't know how to swim. As with everything you do, you must always be careful—whether you're at the beach or in the tub—so you don't get in over your head.

Two baby sisters in Texas, had a terrifying brush

with death in a small pond in their very own backyard. Their entire family quickly learned the hard
way that a peaceful pool of water can turn deadly
in mere seconds!

The McWilliams family lived in a lovely little
trailer park near a small crystal-clear pond surrounded by trees. On a fine, crisp November morning in 1990, the happy family was eagerly packing
up the station wagon to visit Grandma McWilliams
in Houston. Cheryl McWilliams had just returned
from the doctor's office where her two young daughters, two-year-old Nicki and three-month-old Amy,
had had their checkups. Six-year-old Billy, the girls'
older brother, was busy helping their mom load up
the car with everything they would need for a week-
end with grandma.

While Billy and Cheryl bustled back and forth
between their trailer home and the car, Nicki and
Amy stayed buckled into their seats inside the station wagon. They were too young to be of any real
help and Cheryl wanted them to stay put since the
family would be ready to roll very soon.

Finally, Cheryl hopped into the driver's seat and
Billy took his place in the front passenger's seat,
next to his mother. He would be copilot on this trip.
Cheryl had started the car and was about to drive
off when she realized she'd forgotten the roast she
had planned to bring along for dinner. Getting out
of the car again, Cheryl started for the house. Billy
followed close behind to see if he could help.

Since she knew she'd only be a minute, Cheryl

left the car's engine running, but was sure to put the gearshift in the Park position. When the car is in Park, it's supposed to keep the car still until you are ready to drive. But the McWilliams' station wagon was broken. The car did not stay in Park. It began to move; the two little sisters were sitting innocently in the back.

Cheryl and Billy reached the kitchen. Removing the roast from the refrigerator, Cheryl turned to shut the door and return to the car. By chance she looked out the kitchen window and blinked her eyes in disbelief. Surely she wasn't seeing what she thought she saw: There was no one but her little daughters in the station wagon, so it couldn't possibly be driving away—or could it?

Thinking it had to be a dream, Cheryl raced out of the house only to watch in horror as her car, with her two babies in it, picked up speed and steadily rolled down the slope toward the pond. Running faster than she ever had before, Cheryl desperately tried to reach the car before it hit the water. But it was too fast and too heavy for her to stop it, and within seconds, the big automobile made a tremendous splash as it sank into the pond.

The frightened mother leaped into the water along with the car, hitting it with her fists and trying to open the doors to get her girls out. Nicki must have played with the buttons, because the automatic door lock was now on and Cheryl could not open any of the doors. Her kids were trapped inside the sinking car.

Screaming now, Cheryl tried to get Nicki to un-
lock the doors. But the sight of water rising around
the car and her mother's loud voice only scared little
Nicki, who began to cry and move around in the
locked car. Cheryl knew she was frightening her
little girl, but she couldn't help herself. She was
also frightened and could only imagine what would
happen if she didn't get those doors open soon.

Back on the shore, Billy saw what was happening
and although he was afraid for his sisters, he
quickly and calmly dialed 911. The call was immediately transferred and dispatchers Bob Chandler and Sheila Goodman and fire-alarm dispatcher
Steve Hayes were on the line with Billy right away.

The boy was calm, considering the danger his
sisters faced only a few yards away, but he was only
six years old and didn't know his address. The dispatchers, listening to the little boy, tried to piece
together what was happening so they could send
an emergency crew out to help, but they couldn't
seem to locate where Billy lived. Because he kept
saying the car was in the water, they thought he
lived near the ocean or a big lake. The paramedics
and fire fighters were sent out even though they
didn't have the exact address. Billy would just have
to help them find it—quickly.

Out on the pond, the heavy station wagon was
sinking fast. The front end was already underwater
and Cheryl could see it would not be long before the
whole car was filled with water. Her daughters were
very young, and they couldn't swim. If the car sank,

her babies would sink too. This was a terrifying thought and it made Cheryl struggle even harder to try and free her girls.

Unable to break the windows with her fists, Cheryl finally remembered that the back door of the station wagon never locked properly. This was her last chance, her last hope. Swimming around to the back, Cheryl was able to pry open the tailgate, to her great relief. But more trouble was ahead. Her clothes were soaking wet and very heavy. The car was now pointing nose-down into the water, lifting the tailgate high out of the water. Cheryl tried to pull herself up through the rear door, but couldn't get in. Water began to fill the front seat of the car and two-year-old Nicki, feeling the icy water engulf her small body, scrambled over the front seat. The two girls were in the only dry part of the car, Nicki embracing her baby sister Amy. Cheryl, however, was losing strength and couldn't push through the rushing water to rescue her babies.

At that moment, the McWilliams' next-door neighbors, Debbie and Randy Meyers, had looked over and saw the car sinking into the pond. They ran over to see what was wrong. Across the lake, another neighbor, Mike Connolly, heard Cheryl's screams and he too raced over to help.

Mike and Randy dove straight into the water and quickly swam out to the car and Cheryl. Seeing how upset and frightened Cheryl was, they sent her back to shore, where Debbie comforted her.

The two men saw the open tailgate. They also saw

the rising level of water inside the half-submerged car. In a very short time, the whole car would be underwater. If they didn't move fast, Nicki and Amy would be underwater too. They might drown.

In the meantime, Billy was still on the telephone with the dispatchers, with an ambulance already speeding to the scene. But the dispatchers were still having trouble understanding exactly where Billy lived. Because he was only six and the family lived in a trailer park, he couldn't really give them specific directions or even the street address.

The dispatchers were able to tell which town the McWilliams lived in from the telephone computer, but they were depending on Billy to get the emergency crew to the right place. Billy was able to give them some landmarks, some familiar places around his house that helped the crew locate his home, but they hadn't arrived yet. And, as Billy watched the family car sink deeper into the pond, he grew more and more afraid for his sisters.

Out in the pond, Randy Meyers struggled onto the tailgate of the car where he could now see the two frightened girls in the backseat. He reached in and grabbed Nicki, pulled her free and delivered her into the arms of Mike, who was waiting nearby to swim the child to the safety of the shore.

Turning back to the car, Randy now searched for baby Amy. She was no longer in her carseat. The front and back of the car were now completely filled with water. But where was Amy? Was she under all that water? Had she somehow gotten out? Randy was starting to panic as he splashed around the quickly sinking car.

A small sound caught his attention and there, in the corner of the very back, was Amy. Moving with lightning speed now, Randy grabbed the baby and pulled her free of the car just as it went under, totally submerged.

Amy and Nicki were rescued. The car had sunk. And everyone was wet and crying for joy—and gratitude.

Cheryl had now been on the telephone with the dispatchers and, seeing her two babies pulled from the waterlogged car, she screamed and cried hysterically, saying over and over that her children were safe.

Because she was so upset, it was difficult for the dispatchers to understand her. In fact, Bob Chandler, who had been with the EMT for seven years, was glad that young Billy had been on the phone with them all along—he was much more calm and clear than the adults around him. Bob was impressed that the little boy stayed cool in this sticky situation and said, "I think he handled the situation much better than his mother."

In an emergency situation, there are two equally important elements that can save lives—split-second timing and teamwork.

When faced with the possibility of his sisters drowning, Billy had had to make a very quick decision: Should he yell for help at the top of his

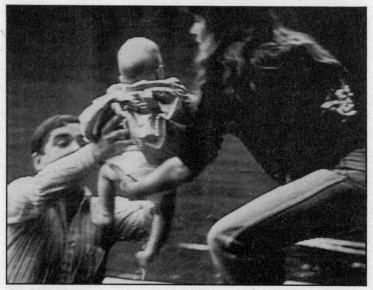

"Randy grabbed the baby and pulled her free of the car just as it went under."

lungs, hoping the neighbors would come, or call 911 for help? Thinking fast, Billy had made the right choice in the blink of an eye. He knew that 911 was the surest way of getting help in an emergency.

In this unusual case, 911 responded as quickly as it could with the confusing directions. And although the emergency team probably would have arrived in time, it was the teamwork of neighbors Randy Meyers and Mike Connolly that had literally saved the sisters' lives.

Once Cheryl McWilliams was sure her daughters were safe, she let all her fear and relief out. There was no sign of the car anymore. The pond had completely swallowed the station wagon. The water's calm surface showed no hint of the tense drama played out just minutes before.

Cheryl hugged Billy, Nicki, and Amy close to her as if she would never let them go again. They were safe.

Cheryl McWilliams had lived through her worst nightmare and knew how lucky she was to have all of her family together. Neighbors Randy and Debbie Meyers and Mike Connolly had been brave and caring. Cheryl felt fortunate to have friends like them.

But perhaps the strongest feeling of all was for her son, Billy. He had always been a big help and a loving son, but in this critical emergency, Billy proved to be a smart, resourceful young man. As soon as he had seen the car moving toward the water, he knew he should call for help.

He was calm, and that helped keep things together. When he picked up the phone, he remembered the numbers 911—probably the most important numbers the McWilliams family will ever know. Billy's steady voice and helpful guidance brought the emergency squad to their home and helped save his sisters.

As Billy said, "I was thinking my sisters wouldn't be alive anymore. The car was leaking and I was thinking that it was sinking and that would be sad for me."

Today there is no sadness in the McWilliams household. The girls are healthy, strong, and happy.

Billy enjoys playing with his little sisters and
Cheryl is proud of her brave family and her quick-
thinking son.

If you are ever faced with a terrible emergency, it
is important to remember those three numbers—
Dial 911.

You can be prepared by remembering the
following:

**KNOW YOUR ADDRESS**—Knowing your
street name, house number, and telephone number
will help an emergency crew find you quickly.

**KNOW A NEARBY NEIGHBOR**—It is a good
idea to know someone who lives near you and might
be helpful in an emergency situation. Go to meet a
neighbor with your parents.

**KNOW WHERE THE EMERGENCY NUM-
BERS ARE KEPT**—Your parents probably have
important telephone numbers posted near the telephone just in case of emergency.

**DIAL 911 FIRST**—Call for emergency help—
dial 911 first—then you can go in search of a neighbor, knowing that help will be there soon.

☆ ☆ ☆

# Girl Shot By Her Own Dad's Gun

Old TV westerns are full of thrilling shoot-outs, the bad guys against the good guys. The bad guys, with their black hats and mean faces, ride into town to cause trouble. It is up to the good guys—you always know them by their white hats—to save the day. The cowboys face each other in the middle of town while the townspeople watch from their hiding places. Guns are pulled out and the bad guy is never quick enough. *Bang! Bang!* Down he goes with his hand over his heart. The good guy always wins.

On television, gunfights are exciting and there is often a reason behind them: The good people have to keep the bad guys out. But in real life, guns are *very* dangerous and thousands of people die every year in accidental shootings. There are often no bad guys or good guys. Anyone—even real people like you—can be shot by accident.

Do you know what a gun looks like or how loud it sounds when it goes off? Maybe you have seen an animal that has been shot. If so, you know that in real life it is not at all like what you see in the movies or on TV. A bullet is so fast, you never see it coming. Once it hits, there is a lot of blood and it really hurts. A bullet can rip you open. It can kill you.

One eight-year-old girl and her eleven-year-old brother know just how scary guns are. They are very lucky to be alive to tell their story.

David and Donna Shore live in a small town in Indiana with their mom and dad. As in many families, both parents work, so after school the two kids would come home, let themselves in, and wait for their parents to finish work. They had been instructed never to leave the house or to let anyone in while they were home alone. The Shores had taught their children to take care of themselves, but they would still call them on the telephone often to check and make sure they were okay.

But there are just some things you can't be prepared for. One summer afternoon, August 1, while the kids' parents were working, David and Donna had invited their friends over to watch TV. The children got bored and started looking for something else to do. David's friend wandered into Mr. and Mrs. Shore's bedroom to see what he might find.

As David followed him in, he saw the boy holding his father's gun—a rifle his dad used when he went hunting.

David knew he was never allowed to play with guns and he told his friend to put it down. But his friend was curious and the gun certainly looked a little more fun than any of the toys he usually played with. David's friend cocked the gun a few times, opening and closing it to point out where the bullets go.

The gun was not loaded but David's friend, who thought he was acting very cool, soon found a bullet nearby and wanted to show how much he knew about guns. He placed the bullet in the gun's chamber, and cocked the gun again.

By now, all the kids had come into the bedroom to see what was happening. "Hey," they said, "it's a real, live gun!" It looked much bigger and scarier than on TV, not at all like the kind Clint Eastwood used in the movies.

Donna yelled at the boy and told him to stop playing with the gun. They all knew it was wrong, so the boy eventually put it back behind the chair where he had found it. He had forgotten one very important thing though: He left the bullet in the gun. Now there was a loaded gun in a house full of children.

The girls went back to their game of dolls, giggling on the Shores' big bed. The older boys wandered off to another part of the house to find their own game. Donna's other friend, a seven-year-old

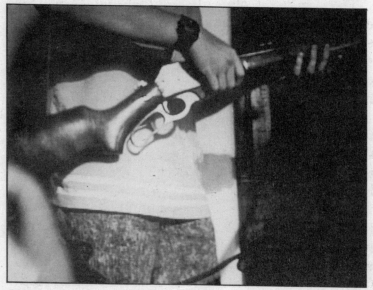

"Now there was a loaded gun in a house full of children..."

boy, felt left out, so he decided he was a big boy and
that he could play with a gun, too. Of course, he
was not such a big boy and a gun is certainly not
a toy. This gun was real—and deadly.

Lifting the rifle, the boy felt how heavy and hard
it was. Thinking he was just as cool as the older
kids, he began to cock the gun the way he had seen
David's friend do it. Over and over again, he opened
and shut the gun's chamber, making a loud *click*
each time. David heard this sound from the other
room and ran into the bedroom to take the gun away
from the child. He was too late.

The gun went off with a sudden *bang*, scaring everyone. The boys were worried that the bullet had somehow damaged the house and they began to search the walls for bullet holes. David was afraid of what his parents would say when they came home and found their bedroom wall blown away.

A small cry from Donna caught everyone's attention. She was lying very still on the bed and there was a big red stain steadily growing larger under her small body. Donna had been shot! She clutched her stomach and groaned in pain.

The children were surprised and just stood there in shock for a minute, not knowing what to do. But it did not take long for the friends to see that they were in big trouble. They ran from the house in fright, leaving young David to take care of his bleeding sister all by himself.

What could he do? His sister was dying right in front of his eyes and he had to think fast to save her life. Telling her she'd be all right and crying himself, David raced to the telephone and dialed 911. He knew he needed help, and he needed it fast. The dispatcher, Michelle Davis, answered immediately and David asked for an ambulance right away. Just as his parents had taught him, David gave the dispatcher his address and telephone number so the emergency crew could find them quickly.

But now he was starting to get really scared and he was fighting back the tears. He kept telling Michelle that his sister was dying, that she had been shot and was bleeding badly. Michelle, hearing how frightened this young boy was, kept him talking on the phone so he would not panic and do something he shouldn't.

Donna was also frightened and confused. Her stomach hurt but she wanted to do something— anything. She heard David on the phone and struggled to walk over to him. The dispatcher told David to keep Donna lying very still. She was not to move around because it might make her injury worse and it was bad enough already.

David wanted to call his mother to let her know what had happened, but the dispatcher kept him on the phone to help him and his sister stay calm. She had her partner call their parents so they could go right to the hospital and meet the children there.

It felt like a year had gone by, but just three minutes after David had made the call to 911, the police arrived at the house. Because the accident had involved a gun, it was important for the police to know just what had gone on that afternoon. They tried to ask David questions, but he was very upset and was only interested in getting his sister some help. The policemen decided their questions could wait until later, until Donna was better.

Two minutes later, the ambulance and paramedics arrived. Just one look at Donna made the paramedics realize how very badly she was hurt. She needed to get to the hospital right away. She had lost a lot of blood and her face was pale and sweaty. Because of the way the bullet went into her body—

through her stomach and out her back, it was a miracle that Donna was still alive.

The paramedics set to work right away, trying to stop the blood and keep it from getting into her wounds. They used special pads for this, put her on a stretcher, and carried her to the ambulance. They drove off, sirens wailing and traffic moving aside, to the hospital.

At the emergency room, Mr. and Mrs. Shore were already waiting to see their little girl. The doctors immediately took her into the operating room to repair her wounds, and see just how badly she was hurt. Although they operated quickly, there was a great deal of blood loss and her liver had been cut right in half. The doctors worked fast but did not think there was much they could do. Now it was up to Donna and her family to be strong for her and to help fight for her life.

The doctors rushed her up to a special part of the hospital just for kids who are very sick or badly hurt. The doctor told Mr. and Mrs. Shore that Donna's chances of pulling through were not good. But her parents never gave up hope. Neither did David, who stayed right at his sister's side and kept telling her to get well.

The whole family stayed close to her during this difficult time. They made sure Donna knew how much they loved her and needed her to come home. It was a tough fight.

The Shores lived from one day to the next, each

day feeling like forever. But only two months after the shooting, Donna was out of the hospital and on her way to the third grade, along with her classmates. Looking at this lively young girl, you would never have known she had come so close to death such a short time ago. Riding her bike, bowling with the family, or just doing her homework, Donna was a lucky girl who was happy to be back to normal.

How did Donna recover? For Donna and her family, it was a matter of hope and luck, as well as David's quick thinking when the accident had happened.

Today David is Donna's hero. He stayed with her every step of the way during that awful time. He saved her life and she will always be grateful. If he hadn't called 911 when he had, if he had tried to call his parents first, it might have been too late to save Donna. Calling 911 is the most important thing you can do—and that is one important lesson you *can* learn from TV.

Getting shot is a very serious thing. As Mrs. Shore said, on TV they make it look like nothing—the doctors just take the bullet out and the person is fine. But the whole Shore family learned an important lesson on that summer day. Real life can be very different from TV. We like to know everything will turn out fine at the end of a TV show, but life isn't a TV show—we don't always know what will happen next.

They say that guns don't kill, people do. But guns

are very dangerous weapons and should never be used as toys. As you know, anything new or unusual is exciting and you might want to get a closer look. We all like to discover new things and sometimes in our excitement, we forget about safety. Unfortunately, some parents forget too, and might put a gun down, just for a moment, in a place you can reach. They forget that their kids like to touch things they are not allowed to and worse, that kids *and* grown-ups can get hurt or even killed when they fool around with guns.

Mr. Shore had not left the gun out for his kids to play with; the gun was strictly for his own use, for hunting. But he never thought it could kill his own baby, one of those he was trying to protect. Sometimes a parent will keep a gun in the home for either protection or for hunting. Usually, these guns are kept in a safe place, out of the reach of young hands. Even so, there are times when you might find yourself face-to-face with a gun.

Have you ever seen a gun up close? What would you do if your sister or brother or friend was shot? You can stay safe by following a few tips that the TV westerns don't tell you:

**STAY AWAY FROM GUNS**—You never know when a gun is loaded.
**HAVE YOUR PARENTS KEEP GUNS AND BULLETS IN A SAFE PLACE**—If they are out of reach, you can't get hurt.

**GET AWAY FAST IF YOU SEE SOMEONE PLAYING WITH A GUN**—You can tell them to put the gun away when you are in a safe place but you don't want to get shot by mistake.

**DON'T MOVE SOMEONE WHO HAS BEEN SHOT**—You don't know where the bullet went and you don't want to make it worse.

**STOP BLEEDING BY PRESSING A THICK TOWEL ON THE WOUND**—If you see where the blood is coming from, get a towel and gently but firmly press it against the wound to try and stop the bleeding.

**KEEP THE VICTIM STILL**—It will only hurt more if the wounded person tries to move.

**DON'T CHECK THE GUN TO SEE WHAT HAPPENED**—If it went off once, it may go off again. Don't be in the line of fire.

**CALL 911 RIGHT AWAY**—Get to a telephone quickly and give the dispatcher your name, address, and telephone number. An ambulance should be there within minutes.

# Mom Gets Help

**H**ave you heard the one about the dog with the sunburn? He was a hot dog!

It's fun to tell jokes and make people laugh. It's also funny to play silly games with your friends or to make up stories and songs. With a little imagination and a good sense of humor, you can turn a boring day into your own party.

There are times, however, when fooling around is not only wrong, but dangerous. Making prank phone calls, for example. Sure, you've heard of people calling numbers and hanging up. But it is not funny to disturb other people with your jokes and it is definitely wrong to tie up the phone lines in case there might be an emergency. And there is nothing more serious than fooling around with 911. That service is there for people who need emergency help—people who could be sick or hurt; people who could be dying.

On July 14, 1990, 911-dispatcher Elisa Peru was on duty in New Jersey. It had already been a long day and the afternoon seemed to drag on endlessly. To make matters worse, Elisa answered a 911 call and instead of hearing an emergency plea, she heard young giggling voices, singing songs and goofing off. She knew this was a prank phone call. And she was mad.

When the line gets tied up with prank calls, real people with real life-or-death emergencies might be trying the number and getting a busy signal. Taking a call and sending help within seconds was what Elisa's job was all about and it just wasn't fair to have these kids abusing the emergency service.

A second prank call came in and Elisa, feeling angry and annoyed quickly tried to get the kids off the phone and at the same time let them know that what they were doing was wrong. Someone's life might depend on it.

By the time her phone rang for the third time, Elisa was fuming. Hearing a little boy's voice on the line made her think this was yet another prank. She was ready to hang up when something in the sound of his voice, some hesitation, and a ring of truth made her stop and listen. Elisa questioned the boy and asked him if he was fooling around. "No," came the insistent reply, "my mama's sick." Elisa knew she had a real emergency on her hands.

Just moments earlier, Paul Bailey, five years old,

had been playing with his younger brother Mike in the backyard. The rowdy boys were hopping and jumping around, just enjoying the warm summer day.

In the house meanwhile, their mother, Ruth Bailey, was talking on the phone with her best friend. A shooting pain suddenly ran through her head and continued right down into her neck. She had never felt such horrible pain and she was caught by surprise. Although Ruth had suffered from diabetes and high blood pressure for the last ten years, she had never felt this kind of alarm. Not wanting to worry her friend and not knowing what was wrong, Ruth got off the phone, saying she was going to check on her kids. She called to them through the window.

Hearing his mother yelling from the kitchen, Paul immediately knew that something was terribly wrong. He sprinted up the back steps two at a time and, breathless, looked inside to find his mother doubled over in pain at the kitchen table. She was throwing up and crying and little Paul was afraid she would die.

Realizing that he had to take control of the situation, Paul remembered his favorite television show, *Rescue 911*, and raced to the phone in the next room to dial those important numbers. He told his mom what he was doing as he placed the call, so she would know everything was going to be okay.

His call went through Elisa, who had just hung up her second prank call of the day. At first unsure of whether this kid was telling the truth or whether the call was just another prank, Elisa listened for a moment to the persistent child. She asked him where he lived, and he gave her all the details.

Although she was still a little uncertain if the call was a real emergency, the turning point came when Elisa asked Paul what floor they lived on. He asked his mother and when Elisa heard Ruth Bailey answer from the background, she knew for sure that this was the real thing. She immediately dispatched an ambulance to the Baileys' house.

Within three minutes, Paul heard the wailing of the sirens as the ambulance sped toward his house. Running outside, he and his brother Mike could see the red lights flashing and they began waving their arms to signal to the driver.

The emergency medical team leaped out of the ambulance and followed Paul into the house. They found Ruth Bailey still vomiting in the kitchen. She was sweaty, pale, and in obvious pain. The crew quickly checked her blood pressure and found it was very high. This might have meant she was having a stroke—a condition in which a blood vessel in the brain either gets blocked or begins to bleed.

It's a little like when a garden hose springs a leak or gets a knot in it. The water can't get through the hose properly. For example, if the hose is attached to a sprinkler, the sprinkler won't work right, or it may even stop altogether. Ruth Bailey's brain, like the sprinkler, was not able to work properly because blood was leaking out of a vein. This is what made her sick.

There was not much the paramedics could do for Ruth at her house, so they put her on a stretcher. Her two scared boys watched wide-eyed from the sidelines. As they wheeled her into the ambulance, Ruth lost consciousness so she couldn't see her boys waving good-bye.

As the emergency vehicle pulled away, the day's events suddenly hit Paul. His mother was very sick and now she had been taken away. He and Mike had never been separated from their mother before. They began to cry for the very first time that day.

A neighbor, Sister Marguritte, who was a nun and knew the kids well, came to stay with the boys while their mom was in the hospital. They did not know how long she would be there.

At Robert Wood Johnson University Hospital, Ruth was given many tests so the doctors could discover exactly what was happening to her brain. They knew one thing though: that she was getting worse as each minute passed. She was very near death.

Doctors put her in a big machine, known as a CAT scanner, which takes pictures of the inside of the brain and shows the doctors what is happening in that mysterious place. Ruth's CAT scan showed that a blood vessel had indeed ruptured deep inside the brain. It was so deep, in fact, that the doctors knew there was no way they could operate to fix it.

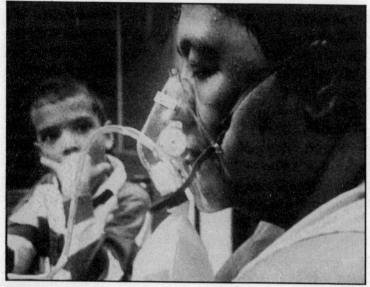

Oxygen masks are standard equipment on most rescue calls.

Ruth had had a brain hemorrhage—her brain was bleeding inside—and it could only be treated with medicine. Now the only hope was that the medicine would work.

Amazingly, the medicine the doctors gave Ruth intravenously—through the veins in her arms to get it directly into her bloodstream—was a huge success. Ruth was awake and talking again within two short days and the entire hospital was thrilled. In three weeks, Ruth was released from the hospital and sent home to her two anxious boys.

Her homecoming was wonderful for the whole

Bailey family. Seeing their mom slowly making her way up the front walk, Paul and Mike flew out the door faster than Superman and were jumping up to hug and kiss their mother. Seeing her again, alive and well, made the boys happier than they had ever been. And, seeing her precious sons for the first time in almost a month, Ruth knew she was blessed with very special children. She knew it was a miracle that she was returning to her family at all, and she hugged the boys even tighter remembering how close to death she had come.

Ruth Bailey knows that her son Paul saved her life by calling 911 so quickly. Ruth is proud of her brave boy and is thankful he paid such close attention to the lessons he learned from the TV show *Rescue 911*.

Dispatcher Elisa Peru is also very proud of Paul. He did the right thing in calling her at 911 and she is glad she listened and was able to get help to his mother in time.

But, as Elisa warns, 911 is a very important number and should *never* be played with. Kids who call it as a prank are not only *not* funny, but they could be causing someone to go without critical emergency help for precious minutes—minutes that can mean life or death.

Remember...

**DO NOT MAKE PRANK PHONE CALLS**—To 911 or to anyone. It is not funny and may be very dangerous.

**SPEAK CLEARLY AND GIVE DETAILS**—If you need to call 911 for an emergency, try to be calm and clear and give the dispatcher as many details as you can.

**TELL THE VICTIM**—Let the person who needs help know that you are calling 911 to keep them calm and assure them that help is on the way.

**911 IS THERE TO HELP YOU**—Use it wisely.

# Behind the Scenes

**C**reating a fast-paced, exciting television show each week takes hard work and lots of talented people.

*Rescue 911* is one of your favorite TV shows because it is filled with action and adventure, heroes and drama. It is in fact based on true life-or-death stories about everyday people.

How does a life-saving rescue end up on a hit TV show?

The producers of *Rescue 911*—the people who put the whole show together—receive close to three hundred letters and phone calls every week from viewers offering story ideas for the show. In addition, a staff of fifteen researchers also calls the 911 centers (the places where the dispatchers receive emergency calls), police departments, fire depart-

Rescuers are often in as much danger as the victims they are rushing to save.

ments, and paramedics across the country looking for stories. From all these sources, researchers narrow down their ideas to the twenty best stories.

These twenty stories are written down, including all the facts and descriptions of what happened, and presented to the producers as a story packet. After reviewing the stories, they choose three to five to become show segments.

Before filming a story, there are several weeks of preparation. The team of producers and researchers assigned to a story will interview all the people who were involved in the rescue. For example, in the

"Best Buddies" story, the production team talked to the Crawford and the Larkin families as well as the police officer, the paramedics, and even the 911-dispatcher who helped make Ricky's rescue a success. This is done so that the show will depict the rescue just the way it happened.

The show's production department makes all the arrangements—hiring the right camera crew, directors, sound experts, and stunt people who can safely and convincingly portray the most dangerous physical aspects of the story. A two-hour production meeting includes about twenty people discussing how to shoot the story, who will be interviewed on camera, and how the stunts will work. Then the film crew takes off for the site of the rescue. In most cases, the crew travels to where the emergency actually occurred.

Now, the filming can begin.

A crew of four to ten people spends about a week shooting nearly twenty hours of interviews and footage—all for a fifteen-minute segment! These tapes are sent overnight to the production offices in Hollywood, California. An editor then views every tape and may spend three to five weeks editing the story until it becomes a short, exciting segment. The segment must be approved by the production company and also by CBS, the television network which airs the show. Three or four segments are used in each episode of *Rescue 911*.

William Shatner, the well-known actor, hosts *Rescue 911* each week. The narration of each story and his on-camera script are written for Mr. Shatner. His part of the show—in which he introduces each segment and then narrates the reenactment—is taped at a real 911 center in Huntington Beach, California.

All the pieces of interviews and reenactments are put in order on videotape. Then the tape is sent to a music composer and a sound effects company where it is "sweetened"—the music, sound effects, and Mr. Shatner's narration are mixed together to create the soundtrack.

Finally, the show is complete. Copies of the tapes are delivered to CBS to air on the network. All that is left now is for you to sit back in your favorite chair, tune in the TV, and join the adventures of real-life heroes on *Rescue 911*. You'll soon be on the edge of your seat!

# GLOSSARY

☆ ☆ ☆

**ACCIDENT**—Something that happens unexpectedly or unintentionally, often unpleasant.

**AMBULANCE**—A vehicle with special medical equipment to transport the sick or injured to the hospital.

**COMA**—A long deep state of unconsciousness usually caused by accident, illness, or injury.

**CONSCIOUS**—Awake, being aware of what is going on around you.

**CONVULSION**—An intense, uncontrollable jerking or irregular movement of the muscles.

**DEXTROSE**—A substance like sugar, made from plant or animal starch, often used as a medicine for people with diabetes.

**DIABETES**—A disease in which the body can't use carbohydrates properly. Associated with too much or too little sugar in the blood or urine. It can cause unusual thirst, hunger, urination, weakness, and, without medical attention, coma and death.

**DISPATCHER**—An operator who takes emergency telephone calls over the 911 line and sends out the proper kind of help, whether it is an ambulance, the police, fire fighters, etc.

**DROWN**—To die by submerging in water or another liquid and being unable to breathe.

**EMERGENCY**—An unexpected situation or sudden urgent event that demands immediate action.

**EMT**—Emergency Medical Team that is dispatched to emergency situations to help injured people.

**ENGULF**—To surround and enclose completely.

**HEMORRHAGE**—To bleed large amounts of blood from the blood vessels.

**INTRAVENOÚSLY**—Through or in the veins, as in receiving medication or liquids directly into the bloodstream through a needle into the vein.

**PARAMEDIC**—A person who is trained to provide emergency medical treatment.

**SUBMERGE**—To place or plunge underwater or another liquid, to cover with water.

**UNCONSCIOUS**—Being unaware of what is going on around you.

☆ ☆ ☆